LIVING IN THE ICE AGE

Elle Clifford
Paul Bahn

Foreword by
Chris Packham

ARCHAEOPRESS

Hand stencils in the cave of El Castillo, Spain

Contents

Foreword iii

Welcome to the Ice Age 1

What did people look like? 10

Where did people live? 12

Case study: Two boys from Sunghir 14

Ice Age food 17

Were people fit and healthy? 22

Did our Ice Age ancestors look after their sick and disabled? ... 28

Making clothes during the Ice Age 30

Jewellery and craftwork 39

Drawing on rocks and cave walls 42

Was every day a play-day or a school-day for children in the Ice Age? 45

Did children have toys to play with? 48

Dogs as hunting aids and pets 51

Are we able to learn anything from our Ice Age ancestors? 56

Archaeological methods 58

Glossary 60

Questions 64

Image credits 66

FOREWORD

When I was a child, the humans described in this book would have been called 'primitive' – such books were about 'primitive man'. Sadly, this painted a very inaccurate description of these people; the word 'primitive' made us think they were unsophisticated, basic, and at an early stage of human evolution. They were portrayed as 'cave men', hairy, naked, grunting, unintelligent animals. But, as you will learn in this wonderful book, this was very wrong – these people were the same as you and I.

Why did we misunderstand the people of the Ice Age? Well, that was down to our own lack of knowledge; but now, thanks to scientists and new technologies, we have learned so much more. They were far from primitive, they were clever, resourceful and inventive – they needed to be to survive in some very difficult environmental conditions. They were also skilful and creative, making beautiful clothes and tools, even what might have been toys for their children. Perhaps most importantly they were adaptable, learning to live and survive in many different habitats and conditions.

This fascinating book also shows us how they thrived, day to day – how they dressed, their jewellery, their shelters, what they ate, their health and diseases, how they looked after their families and their dogs, even what they looked like.

It's tempting to think that we can learn little from people who ate and drank, laughed and cried, between 40,000 and 12,000 years ago, but I think we should – because these remarkable people not only lived but survived through a period of unimaginable change on our planet. And now, once again, our planet is changing, this time because of our activities. And it's changing more quickly, more dramatically, than it did for these Ice Age humans; but if these ancient families survived, then we can survive too.

Chris Packham
Naturalist, Broadcaster and Environmental Campaigner

Reconstruction of an Ice Age woman and child

Welcome to the Ice Age

Journey with us back to the Last Ice Age, and discover how small communities lived a **hunter-gatherer lifestyle** during this long time period of our ancient history. You will find out about:

- the different types of homes that Ice Age communities lived in;
- how they **foraged** and hunted for the resources they needed to survive in an ever-changing landscape;
- how our ancestors could craft fine tools and objects, and make beautiful art and jewellery;
- how their way of life had little impact on the environment in which they lived.

The period of time we will be referring to as the Last Ice Age is also called the 'Upper Palaeolithic' or 'Upper Old Stone Age'. It may have been one of the most important stages in human history, and the scientists who have studied this early part of our existence have produced evidence for what seem to be dramatic changes in our thinking, behaviour and development. Learning about our complex and exciting past gives us a greater understanding of the way **foraging** people manage their environment. This can help us to appreciate our planet and have a better understanding of what it means to be human.

50,000 years ago

Modern humans in Europe

40,000 years ago

Neandertals become extinct in Europe

30,000 years ago

Last Ice Age / Upper Palaeolithic /

22–20,000 years ago
Glacial Maximum, long winters!

DEEP TIME LINE

Time line from the approximate arrival of modern humans in Europe to the present

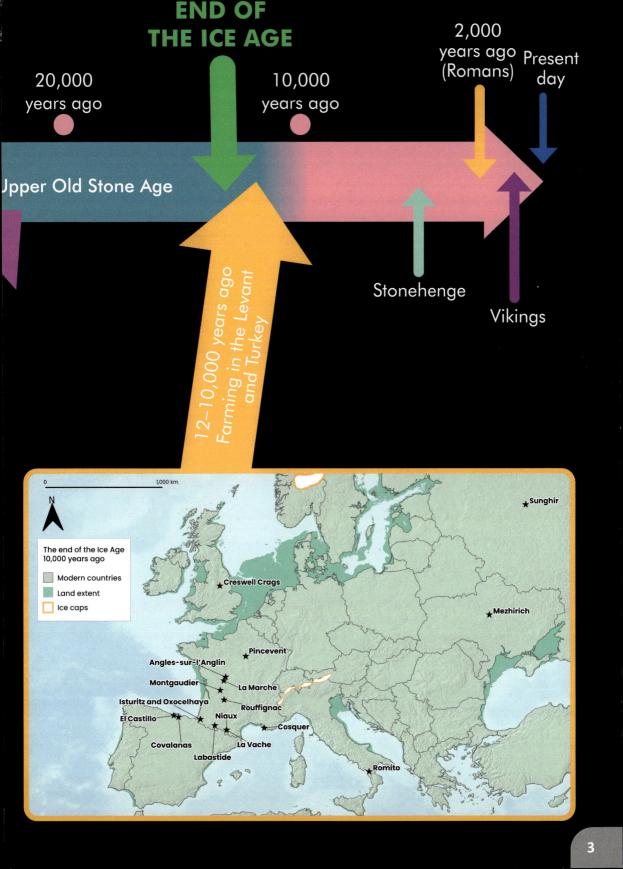

Engraving of cave lions from La Vache, France. Ice Age lions do not seem to have had manes!

The people you will meet in this book lived in Europe during the Ice Age. Many living here today are their direct descendants. Humans have always moved about our planet, from even before the Ice Age to the present day, and often over great distances, so our present population is also made up of the descendants of those who were living in other parts of the world at that time. The people we are learning about are called **biologically modern humans** (also known as *Homo sapiens*) – that means they are just like us. They were every bit as intelligent as we are, they just didn't have the knowledge we have gained since their time. Their culture and lifestyle were very different to those we take for granted today. They lived from around 40,000 years ago to 12,000 years ago when the Last Ice Age came to an end, and most (but not all) of our early ancestors eventually became farmers. There are around 10 million people alive today who still live a hunter-gatherer lifestyle in very

different parts of the world. Some live in desert-like conditions in Africa and Australia, others herd reindeer in Siberia. Many **indigenous/first nations** people live in Canada and the Arctic, and others in the rainforests.

We know that people living during the Ice Age were very good at inventing all sorts of things to help them survive the difficult conditions they had to deal with. As far as we know, Ice Age humans – our direct ancestors – living thousands of years ago, had no written language or way of telling the time, or of measuring things like we do. You might wonder how they managed to organise themselves and plan for the future without the things we take for granted. And most importantly, how could they teach the next **generation** everything they needed to know in order to survive an ever-changing climate and environment?

Wild ox engraved at Romito, Italy

We will be going back in time tens of thousands of years to find out how these ancient people lived – obviously lots of them must have survived, or we wouldn't be here today! Many of the things they learned to do we still do today, and it's fascinating to think that some of our knowledge and many of our skills have been directly handed down from parents to their children by word of mouth for well over a thousand generations. That only changed when we invented a written language, and people could write all their knowledge and stories down.

Our Ice Age ancestors were resourceful people who survived at a time when it wasn't cold all of the time but it was colder than it is now in Europe – generally 5 or 6 degrees lower than today!

They had to cope with rapid changes in the climate which altered the landscape around them, the vegetation, and the animal life they were able to hunt. At times these great changes would have led to animal **migrations**, and as a consequence humans would follow. This may have led them to alter some aspects of their way of life – and even the type of tools they needed to use.

During the last Ice Age, people lived in extended family groups, and children would have made up a large part of those communities. Hunter-gatherer people, both in the past and those living today, have a different way of life to our modern western society, where an 'immediate' or 'nuclear' family structure of two parents and children is more common.

An extended family structure means that child-rearing responsibilities extend beyond the immediate family group to aunts, uncles, cousins and grandparents, for example. There are strong bonds between family members. Also, in some foraging communities, children are considered to be the responsibility of all the adults, who together teach children their values, customs, how to behave towards others, and very importantly, the skills they need to survive. Being 'a good parent' is highly valued in these indigenous communities, and they also take responsibility for looking after their sick, disabled and old people.

To help us get a better understanding of what life was like for families living during the Ice Age, let's take a look at the jobs adults needed to do to ensure their own and their children's survival. It's both a myth and a silly notion that these early communities had lots of spare time – our Ice Age ancestors would have been very busy during the daylight hours – and even young children would have learned to be useful from a very early age, just like hunter-gatherer children living today.

Many children's activities would have helped them learn everything they needed to survive, like:

- making fires for warmth and cooking;
- sheltering from freezing temperatures;
- recognising when food was spoiled or poisonous;
- how and where best to track and hunt animals;
- and making sure they could find their way home without a map!

It is probable that children will also have learned how to make a basic set of tools. In the Ice Age countless stone tools were made, primarily of sharp flint when it was available – scrapers, knives, perforators, etc. Implements were also made of bone, antler and mammoth ivory. There were probably also many tools of wood and other organic materials, but these have not survived.

Many tasks would have been seasonal, so they would have had to devise ways of anticipating the changes in the climate, the migration of herds, etc., and get prepared in advance.

It is also a myth that hunting was the most important occupation during the Last Ice Age, as there were many other vital jobs to do. People would have made their homes near rivers or streams as fresh water would need to be collected regularly – humans can only survive an average of 3 days without water. It is unlikely that everyone went to the river every time they needed a drink, so we can assume that at some point these early humans learned to make containers that stored large amounts of water. Where there

A pile of animal dung fuel in a village in India. Ice Age people may have burned dung too!

are rivers and streams there are also fish, and animals coming to drink: this would provide the opportunity for someone to lie in wait, and seize any unsuspecting creature that came along to the water's edge.

Apart from collecting water, finding enough wood for their fires would be a priority. Archaeologists have found the remains of countless ancient fires and hearths in rock shelters and caves – these would have been used for lighting, warmth, cooking, and keeping away dangerous predators such as cave lions.

During warm phases of the Ice Age, there would have been plenty of trees and bushes to provide wood, but in cold phases some regions would have had very few trees or none at all

When wood was in short supply, people would have burned animal bones and even animal dung. But neither of these would have been pleasant options inside a rock shelter, as both create very stinky thick smoke.

What did people look like?

How can we know what people looked like? There are two methods: first, we have skeletons, which tell us that they were about the same size as ourselves – men were an average of 1.8m (5 ft 9 in) tall, and women 1.66m (5ft 4in). The bones also show us that they were tough, robust people, with well-developed muscles, especially in the legs. And skeletons can also indicate how old they were when they died – with examples from newborn infants to people in their 60s. If their skulls are well-preserved, then scientific artists are able to reconstruct the faces, giving us reasonably accurate portraits, although of course many aspects can only be guesswork – the shape and size of noses and ears, the colour of eyes and hair, the presence or absence of beards and moustaches, and the length and style of hair.

An artist's reconstruction of a woman who lived during the last period of the Ice Age

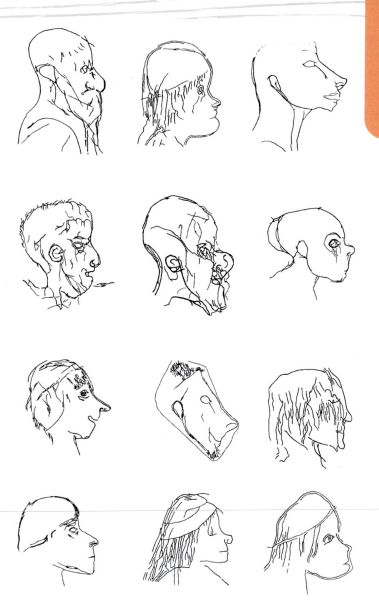

Some of the human portraits engraved at La Marche, France

Fortunately, however, there were also artists in the Ice Age, and they have provided us with the second source of our knowledge. Although they mostly drew animals, they were also capable of illustrating people, and one site, La Marche in France, has produced numerous such engravings on slabs of stone. They show us a whole gallery of characters from about 17,000 years ago. As you can see, they looked just like us!

Where did people live?

Although we often talk about 'cave men', Ice Age people did not live inside caves – which can be wet and unpleasant. Instead they lived in cave entrances (as in those of Creswell Crags in Britain), and in sunny rock shelters. They also lived in the open-air, using tents and huts – these disappeared long ago, but we can tell their shapes and sizes from the fireplaces and rubbish left inside and around them. In some parts of central and eastern Europe, where mammoth bones were plentiful, they even built huts out of mammoth skulls, jaws, tusks and other huge bones.

A recreation of a mammoth bone hut at Mezhirich, Ukraine. It was probably covered with skins, or perhaps wood or turf.

In some sites, hundreds of small stone slabs were collected and laid down as a kind of pavement. Scientists have also found pollen in soil samples which show that grasses and flowers were sometimes brought into homes, presumably for bedding and seating. In one German cave, the amount of fat in the soil indicated that the floor was probably covered in the skins of large mammals, while in the Spanish cave of La Garma there is evidence that the skin of a cave lion was used as a mat!

It is clear that Ice Age people had base camps (some seasonal, others permanent), as well as minor hunting camps. One good example is at Pincevent in France where, about 13,000 years ago, we have evidence that hunters visited at least 15 times, always between April and October – to prey on migrating herds of reindeer. They lived in light and movable tents which they took with them when they moved on. It is thought that 35 reindeer hides would have been needed for each tent's covering (over a structure of wooden poles). Each tent could shelter 4 or 5 people, and it is thought that about 11 of them formed this temporary village of around 50 people. The **debris** they left behind shows clearly the areas where flint tools were made, skins were processed and food was cooked. At other sites one can see evidence for the making of tools, beads and art objects in bone, antler and ivory.

A recreation of a Pincevent tent

Case study: Two boys from Sunghir

Some 25,000 years ago, two boys were buried at a hunting site at Sunghir (in present day Russia). The boys were aged around 12 and 10, and although they were buried together, they were not related to each other.

They probably wore clothing made of reindeer skins, with the thousands of tiny ivory beads found in the grave sewn onto their garments and hoods. Lines of beads along the legs, round the knees and ankles, and on the feet indicate that their trousers were sewn to their shoes. On the older boy, 250 fox canine teeth (a fox has only 4 canines) were attached to what must have been a belt.

The younger boy found in the burial had unusually short and bowed femurs (upper leg bones) which may have caused him some pain or difficulty in walking. However, the bones of his upper body were extremely sturdy, indicating that he perhaps worked hard at a demanding task that involved a sitting position. As a very young boy he may have needed quite a lot of carrying around.

When the older boy's teeth were examined in the laboratory there was almost no wear on them, and his lower jaw would have had little bite force, indicating he would have had great difficulty chewing meat. Usually, teeth recovered from the Ice Age show a great deal of wear from eating **fibrous** and gritty foods. People dug **tubers** and roots from underground, and probably didn't bother to wash off the soil and grit, and over time this would have caused tooth damage.

Reconstructed image of the boys' clothing and jewellery at the Sunghir burial

However, scientific analysis of the boy's bones revealed he did not lack protein in his diet. So, we can only conclude this must have come from invertebrates such as earthworms, insects, spiders, snails and slugs. Yum!

Ice Age Food

We need to eat 13 million calories of food from infancy to the age of eighteen. That is around 250,000 apples! That is a lot of food to find, and it is likely that at times food would have been in very short supply. The amount of food that could be stored would be limited, although people probably dried leftover meat and fish, and even froze food when the snow and ice were thick enough. Food would have to have been stored carefully so that other animals couldn't come along and help themselves!

Feeding the Ice Age Family

The most important requirement for Ice Age communities would be to ensure they had enough food every day to feed everyone. This would involve the following tasks:

- Hunting and butchering animals
- Catching small animals like rabbits in nets or traps
- Catching and gutting fish
- Gathering seasonal foodstuffs: roots, plants, small berries and nuts, and when available, bird eggs from nests
- Preparing and cooking food like meat, fish and bone marrow

Would you have enjoyed learning the skills you'd need to make food in the Ice Age?

The food available to our early ancestors would have depended greatly on the climate at any given time – and this differed widely over the many thousands of years of the Last Ice Age and the different regions and habitats. For example, it was much colder along the northern coast of Spain, where people must have been good at harpooning fish from the sea, and even catching seals.

What animals were available to hunt, or fish, depended on the migration habits of various species throughout the different seasons. We also know that people moved from site to site, and had more than one home base. This was probably to lessen the chances of hunting any animal to **extinction**, and running out of local resources. Small game like rabbits and birds could fill in as reliable food stuffs during periods when there was nothing else to hunt. We can assume that our Ice Age ancestors did everything they could to manage their food resources, and it is unlikely they ever wasted a mouthful of food. The discarded animal bones found at cave sites that have been examined by **archaeologists** have had every scrap of meat and marrow removed!

Drawing of a woolly mammoth in Rouffignac cave, France

Foods available in Ice Age Europe

- Reindeer, red deer, megaloceros (giant deer), ibex, chamois, horse, bison, moose, woolly mammoth, rhino and saiga antelope
- Small mammals: rabbits and hares
- Birds (and their eggs), waterbirds
- Sea and river fish
- Seals, marine fish, crustaceans, shellfish and seaweed
- Molluscs (limpets and periwinkles), oysters, clams, mussels
- Invertebrates: woodlice, worms, slugs and snails
- Nuts, berries, rhubarb, some fruits, weeds, plant foods and fungi
- Wild cereal grains

Would you rather hunt for and gather your food every day or go to the supermarket?

An Ice Age engraving of a hare on stone from Isturitz, France

What food our ancestors ate can tell us a great deal about how healthy they were, although it is impossible to know how reliable their food supply was from one season to the next. People must have often worried about food shortages. This could have been the result of the climate getting harsher, animals changing their patterns of migration, or plants and tubers failing to grow, leaving families and communities without enough to eat. Periods of starvation are likely to have occurred over the many thousands of years of the Last Ice Age, and the people who survived were likely to be very strong and tough – their ancient 'hardy genes' have been passed down to us, so we have a lot to thank them for! Also, they probably learned the benefits of sharing their food with other families who would return the favour in the future. It is probable that Ice Age people

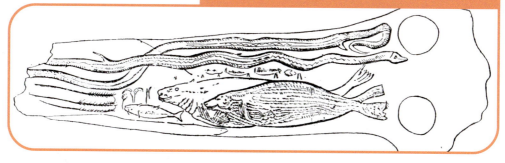

Marine mammal scene of seals, fish and eels engraved on an antler, from Montgaudier cave, France

ate everything that was available and possible to eat – they may even have eaten **putrefied** (rotting) food. Indeed, some modern hunter-gatherers find rotten food a delicacy – with or without accompanying maggots!

It is likely that everyone learned to hunt – including children; and men and women, children and the elderly collected anything and everything that was available to eat. Children would have practised chasing and catching small animals just as hunter-gatherer children do today. Ice Age children would certainly have learned how to butcher animals and extract marrow from the bones. This is not an easy task and youngsters probably started with small animals like rabbits and hares before tackling bigger animals like deer.

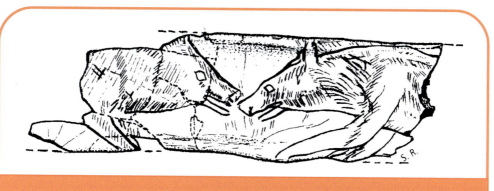

Wolves engraved on a bone, from La Vache, France

Were people fit and healthy?

Our early ancestors were certainly active and had to be physically fit to survive. Adults and children had to walk everywhere to collect food, water, wood, and stone for their tools. They needed to run fast to chase prey, and walk and climb over rugged hilly terrain to collect and carry everything back to their home-base. This would certainly have built up strong bones and powerful muscles. But it must have been a tough life when people became injured or old, especially when they needed to drag heavy loads to the next camp site or rock shelter. Butchering large animals with the tools they had, and preparing animal hides involve hard manual labour. However, Ice Age people were not necessarily super-healthy just because they were fit!

Reconstruction of an Ice Age woman during pregnancy

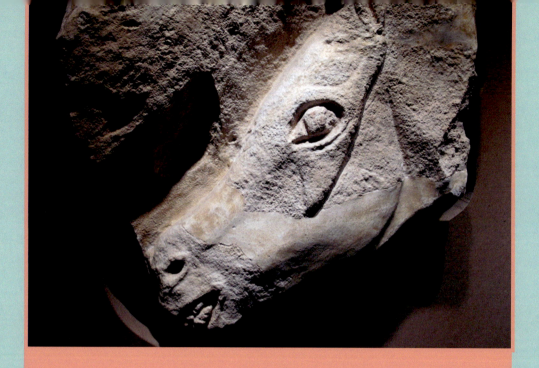

Sculpted head of a horse from Angles-sur-l'Anglin, France

Many of the diseases we encounter today appeared when humans started **domesticating** animals and began farming. But this didn't happen until the end of the Last Ice Age around 12,000 years ago. Also, even though we have no idea how many people were alive during the Last Ice Age, it is probable that people lived in relatively small communities so as not to over-**forage** or over-hunt the animals in their local area, or use up important resources like wood. Another reason why populations did not grow large over thousands of years is that hunter-gatherer people tend to have small families – perhaps only two or three children at most. This is because it takes a great deal of effort to raise children to adulthood, especially hunter-gatherer children. Remember, it requires 13 million calories for an infant to get to 18 years of age!

Parasitic infections such as flatworms and tapeworms would have almost certainly been present in our ancestors' guts. If the older boy from Sunghir acquired his protein from slugs and worms, it would have increased his chances of parasitic infections. Researchers have found the eggs from parasitic intestinal roundworms from faecal material (poo) in soil samples in a cave in northern France. It could have been left there by a cave bear (they visited this same cave), but scientists are almost certain the eggs were in human excrement. One thing our Ice Age ancestors had not learned to do was wash their hands before eating food!

Fungal infections. The cold conditions made it necessary for Ice Age people to be continuously dressed in animal-hide clothing, but this is not without possible health hazards! Parasites and fungal infections can be transferred to humans in a variety of ways, and even slight infections can leave marks on human bones, and especially young children. The older boy from Sunghir had traces of infection (*Mycosis fungoides*) on his spine that probably started as a skin infection.

Head and body **lice** like to hang out on humans (in clothing, hair and even beards and eyebrows) and were almost certain to be regular visitors on our Ice Age ancestors' bodies. Recent research suggests that lice as well as gut worms can help humans boost their immunity against **pathogens**. So perhaps having creepy-crawlies inside their trousers helped our ancestors to stay healthy!

When people started using fire to cook, the smoke, ash and dust could have contributed to lung diseases such as Tuberculosis (TB) and even some cancers. Fires – especially ones that were burning bones – would have been bad for the health of infants and children

LOVELY AROMAS OR TERRIBLE ODOURS?

Would our Ice Age ancestors have found each other smelly? We can probably assume they smelled differently to us, and more like the animals whose skins they fashioned into warm clothing. Maybe they even found this smell pleasant! Personal hygiene probably wasn't important to them, and it is unlikely being dirty had any lasting effect on their health, because even as babies they would have developed lots of immunity to most of the **pathogens** that would make us ill today. People may have washed in rivers or used snow to clean themselves when available, but alternatively, they may have not felt it necessary.

If our Ice Age ancestors had a word for smelly, what do you think it would be?

in particular. Smoke is filthy, as it clings to clothing and hair. Perhaps this is one reason why they didn't live inside caves but preferred cave mouths and rock shelters.

Our bodies have also **evolved** ways of fighting disease: one example is a mother's milk which provides **antibodies** that are transmitted directly to the infant's gut to protect it against a range of parasitic and harmful infections – and as we mentioned earlier, it's probably safe to assume that parasites would have been present in our ancestors' guts! They ate animals, and not all of the meat would have been cooked well enough to kill bacteria, and it's also possible that they ate the contents of various animals' stomachs too and food that was putrefied (going bad). Apparently, some modern Arctic hunter-gatherers consider rotten seal flippers something of a delicacy to eat!

Even though we don't know how much immunity Ice Age people had to infections, or what germs were around, it's highly unlikely that they suffered from the whole range of food allergies known today, or that they were allergic to animals or 'cave dust'. Modern standards of cleanliness and using disinfectants has resulted in many people today having overactive **immune systems**.

It is probable that these early communities had learned that some plants could be used as medicines, and had remedies for a number of health problems. Of course, this would be dependent on the availability of suitable plants in their local environment. Certainly, **iodine** can easily be extracted from seaweed, and the iron-rich rock haematite (red ochre) was used extensively throughout prehistory – even before our own species *H. sapiens* came on the scene – for its cleansing and **antiseptic** qualities.

Do you think we are all too clean?

Would you prefer to wash less?

This antler carving from southern France may be the only depiction of poo in the Ice Age. It shows a fawn (baby deer) turning back to look at two birds sitting on its over-sized poo. This strongly implies that Ice Age people, like us, had a sense of humour!

OTHER POSSIBLE ILLNESSES OR CAUSES OF DEATH DURING THE LAST ICE AGE COULD BE:

- Starvation and lack of essential minerals and vitamins
- Accidents and injuries like broken bones or wounds leading to infections
- Hypothermia or frostbite
- Evidence of mouth and gum infection has been found on Ice Age skeletons

There is little evidence of violence or wars in the Ice Age – this is probably because people needed to co-operate with each other, and help other communities in times of need. Trading goods and materials like desirable flint for their tools with people in other areas would have encouraged good relations, just like having good trading partners in different parts of the world today. For example, we don't grow bananas or coconuts in Great Britain, so we have to be on good terms with people in other parts of the world who can send them to us.

It is unlikely that people in distant communities spoke the same language, so do you think they may have shared a 'sign' language or other ways that helped them communicate with each other?

Did our Ice Age ancestors look after their sick and disabled?

To date, archaeologists have only discovered a couple of hundred burials from the Ice Age, and a small number of those burials have contained children or adults that had disabilities. This suggests our ancestors were very caring and compassionate people who supported people in the community who needed help to survive, and who could not contribute as much as others to the daily workload.

The remains of a person were discovered in a rock shelter in Italy, and the excavators that found the skeleton called him Romito. He was probably a young male (though without DNA testing we can't be sure), and was around 16–18 years of age when he died. This young person was of short height (around 4'2"), and all of his long bones were bowed and deformed and about half the size of average limbs, a condition usually associated with dwarfism.

It is thought that the most likely cause of Romito's dwarfism was a **genetic mutation,** and he is the only example we have of this condition in an Ice Age hunter-gatherer society. One would expect this to be a very rare condition 11,000 years ago – and given the small population sizes at the time, it's unlikely to have been encountered often.

Romito would have had difficulty walking and travelling any distance without assistance, and it is also unlikely that he could have used the weapons needed to hunt, as his forearms were extremely short and bowed, and he would have had difficulty bending his elbows. In order to survive from early childhood, Romito was probably given support to manage his disabilities. We can only guess what skills and talents he may have developed as part of his community.

For a mobile hunter-gatherer group, migrating to other sites is a necessity, and it cannot have been easy for Romito to keep up with the others, without enduring a great deal of pain. Only with the support and protection of his extended family could Romito have managed to survive into early adulthood.

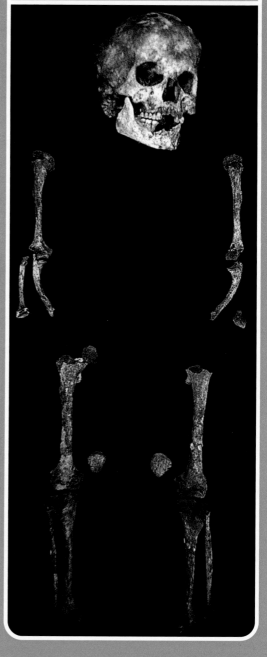

The Romito boy's skeleton

Making Clothes during the Ice Age

Making sure that everyone (especially infants and children) had suitable clothing would have been a major job for the men, women and children in the community. This is the same today for modern hunter-gatherer people like the Inuit, who live in regions round the North Pole, and need to wear warm animal skins to keep out the freezing temperatures. The main hunting season for our ancestors would be during the summer months, and it's most likely that the preparation and sewing of animal skins would have been undertaken in the autumn, when families relied on trapping smaller animals for food.

When we stop to think about the protective clothing people needed during the Last Ice Age, it is staggering how much skill and labour would have been required to make the outfits they needed

Things people made in the Ice Age

- Preparing animal skins and furs for clothing
- Making textiles for clothing, ropes, and nets
- Making containers from animal skins and plant materials
- Collecting stone, bone and antler, and ochre for tools
- Ochre for painting and medicinal purposes
- Making tools like needles and awls for sewing clothing, beads and jewellery

to keep out sub-zero temperatures. Even animal skin clothing wears out, and they probably needed to replace their clothing every year, which would have taken up a great deal of time.

The invention of clothing probably came about as the climate in

Textile imprint on the wall of Cosquer cave

Europe grew colder and humans needed to protect themselves from the severe weather conditions. Fitted clothing made of animal hides can trap body heat inside and give the wearer protection from the wind, cold and from getting wet. Ice age Europe had an average temperature 5 or 6 degrees lower than it is today, similar to that of present-day Norway and Sweden.

As the climate cooled, it probably forced people to migrate southwards to find warmer places to live. During the warmer summer months simpler or lighter outfits would have been worn, but during glacial conditions clothing that gave **thermal protection** would have meant the difference between life and death, especially for children and infants. It is probable that people carried tools like needles around with them in case they needed to do any quick repairs to their clothing. It takes lots of time to produce wearable animal hides and make clothing, and it is likely this was done at a particular time of the year when there was still some sunshine and

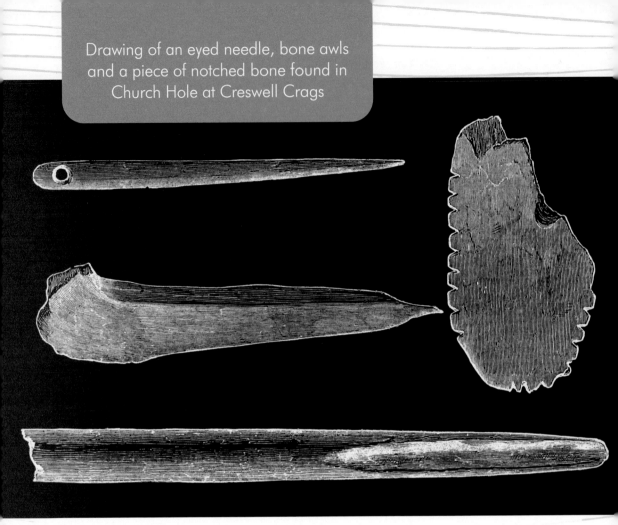

Drawing of an eyed needle, bone awls and a piece of notched bone found in Church Hole at Creswell Crags

enough daylight hours to work outside. Skin preparation requires some sunlight, so the winter would have been too cold for the processing treatment to be a success. It's also worth noting that animal hides (and furs) would be at their thickest in the winter and hence involve more work.

Many bone and antler tools were probably used for skin working – **spatulas, smoothers, shuttles** – and wooden tools were also used, but have mostly now disintegrated (rotted) so are very rarely found. It is very likely that both adults and children would have learned how to process skins, and produce effective clothing and footwear.

HOW TO PREPARE AN ANIMAL SKIN FOR CLOTHING

1. Peg-out an animal skin, or tie it to a wooden frame to stretch it, before scraping off all the muscle tissue and fat from the internal surface with the edge of a scraper.

2. Remove all the hair by 'sweating' the skin over a few days: the natural bacterial decay loosens the hair at the roots.

3. Repeatedly soak, wash and 'work' the skin.

4. Place the skin against a large log or stone, and scrape away the hairs* with a blunt-edged tool.

5. The hide is then dried in the sun to '**cure**'; then it needs further soaking, working, wringing and drying until the material is soft (working consists of pummelling, scraping, and hand-pulling in all directions as it dries).

6. Drying might have been assisted by 'smoking' the skin over a slow, smouldering fire made from rotten wood under a makeshift skin tent. This sterilizes and makes skins supple.

7. Skins can be waterproofed by rubbing the surface with cooked animal fat.

* The animal hairs recovered from hides could be turned into felt material – this involves working the hairs together with one's hands or feet, a simple task that anyone could do. Alternatively, the hairs could be made into strings for netting or cordage; and bristles could be used to make brushes, which were used to make some cave paintings.

Would you have enjoyed making your own clothes in the Ice Age rather than buying them like we do today?

It has been estimated that it takes 300 hours of work to treat the 27 reindeer hides needed to make enough clothing for a family of five people – including inner and outer parka, mitts, boots, stockings, etc. Such an outfit would last two years at best, and is usually replaced every year due to wear and tear. This does not take into account hides needed for sleeping bags, or making sleighs, tents, etc. If clothing is made from small animals like foxes, a truly huge number of skins is needed, and this entails lots of work in trapping, skinning, **tanning**, sewing, and so on.

Once treated, the skins would have been made into clothing and shoes, as well as used in tents and huts. It is extremely probable that early groups had a waste-not-want-not approach to life, as skin preparation involved a great deal of time and effort. Indeed, it's likely that 'recycling' old goods probably started in the Ice Age. When clothing became worn-out or uncomfortable, or was infested with lice, the old hides would have probably been used in some other way. For example, old skins might be sewn together and hung over a rock shelter opening in order to keep out the wind and cold, as well as night predators. They could also be made into blankets, sleeping bags, roof covers and tents, slings for carrying infants, or manufacturing small canoe-type boats, or vessels for liquids or cooking. Some animal guts could have been used as waterproof linings, while their bladders make excellent bags for carrying or storing liquids. People almost certainly had ways of preserving and storing food over the winter although almost all the containers they used were made of materials that rot and so have not survived over such long periods.

Although no actual clothing has survived from the Last Ice Age, lots of the tools, such as awls and needles, that people used to process

The Muraba'at basket is around 10,500 years old

hides and make clothing have been recovered by archaeologists. When these ancient tools are examined using a microscope, scientists can see marks which show they have been in contact with animal hides.

Archaeologists have now realized that weaving and basketry must also have been of great importance in the Last Ice Age. Although no actual woven materials have been found, impressions of textiles made from wild plants have been found on fragments of fired and unfired clay. They show a wide variety of techniques and styles, with eight different types of string from plant materials. It is probable that Ice Age people used both hides and woven products for nets to catch small animals, for bags, blankets and matting on the floor as well as a way to keep out draughts from their rock shelters.

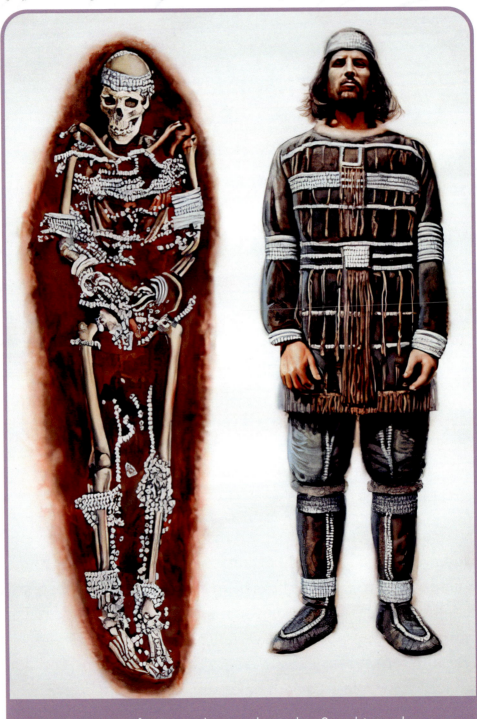

Drawing of a man who was buried at Sunghir, and a reconstruction showing what his clothes might have looked like.

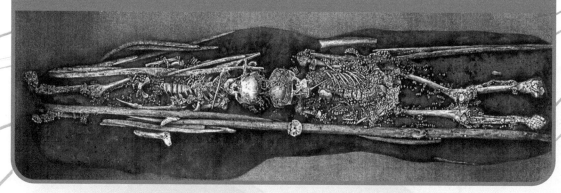

Drawing of the two Sunghir boys' remains. There were over 10,000 beads made of mammoth tusk ivory on the children's clothing found in the grave. It is estimated to have taken more than 3,500 hours of expert work to produce that number of beads.

According to reconstructions by archaeologists, people who lived in cold climates would have worn fur coats very similar to the clothes of people living in the Arctic today, with long trousers, moccasin-type footwear or boots, and a poncho-style overcoat. These may have been fastened with ivory buckles or bone buttons and decorated with lots of ivory beads, as seen in the burials at Sunghir.

Since humans can't walk barefoot in snow or on ice, moccasin-type shoes or boots with rigid soles, or sandals in the summer, were almost certainly worn throughout the Ice Age. These could have been made using animal hides, even rabbit and fish skins, or perhaps tree bark cut into strips and woven together. Dry moss could have been used to make the insides comfy.

Little human figures made from mammoth ivory, found in the Lake Baikal region of Siberia and dating back to the Ice Age, show them wearing belts, headgear, buttons, bracelets, shoes, backpacks, and all-in-one overalls or 'onesies.'

The numerous bones of arctic fox, red fox, wolverine and wolf found at sites in Russia and Siberia imply that the people were hunting these animals for their furs, which are the warmest and most effective coverings for keeping out the cold.

Infants might have been swaddled (wrapped tightly) and then placed and strapped onto a wooden plank, or attached to a basket made from woven fibres. Dried grass and moss could be placed at the bottom of the pouch to act as a nappy. Swaddling would also restrict the infant's movements so it couldn't crawl off or get into danger, and it is safe from predators if high above the ground. For journeys to other camp sites, larger travel baskets or **cradleboards** could be secured to a sled used to transport older children who were unable to walk quickly enough to keep up with the group.

Russian figurines made from mammoth ivory – they could have been children's playthings

Jewellery and craftwork

Long before the beginning of the Ice Age people started making and wearing jewellery from shells, teeth, bits of bone and animal antler. We know this because archaeologists have discovered a few spectacular Ice Age burials where the jewellery made of ivory, shells or animal teeth has remained long after the clothing it was attached to has disappeared.

Necklace from Labastide cave, France: the engraved bone pieces would probably have been strung together through the pierced holes with twine or hairs from a horse's tail.

Around 100 years ago, archaeologists discovered a 12,000 year old burial of a child aged between 2 and 4 in the Dordogne area of France. Over 1,500 shells were found around the arms, legs, neck and the head of the child's remains and must have been attached to a garment or a wrap. Pendants made of fox and deer teeth were also in the grave.

Do you think beads were worn every day, or just for special occasions like ceremonies, or perhaps only for burial?

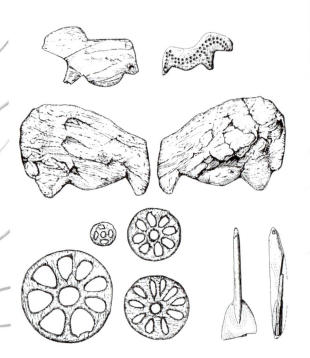

Some of the ivory carvings found with the Sunghir burials

Do you believe that lucky charms can stop bad things from happening?

The shells showed evidence of wear, and they had been cut down to make them smaller, so it is possible they may have been worn previously by members of the child's family or community before being given as **grave goods**. This may have been simply to create a lasting connection between the child and those still living that loved them, but there is an alternative theory. Some modern **foraging** people living in the Amazon cover their children's clothing with lucky charms to protect them from 'bad spirits', but if the child dies then the charms are believed to be useless and cannot be passed on, so they are buried along with the child.

Some of the shells came from very far away, and must have been acquired through trading with people who collected them along the seashore. It used to be thought that this child or its parents must have been important members of their community. We now have a better understanding of **indigenous** peoples' beliefs, and ornaments and goods reflect people's affection for each other, rather than only showing value or status.

The shells from the La Madeleine child burial

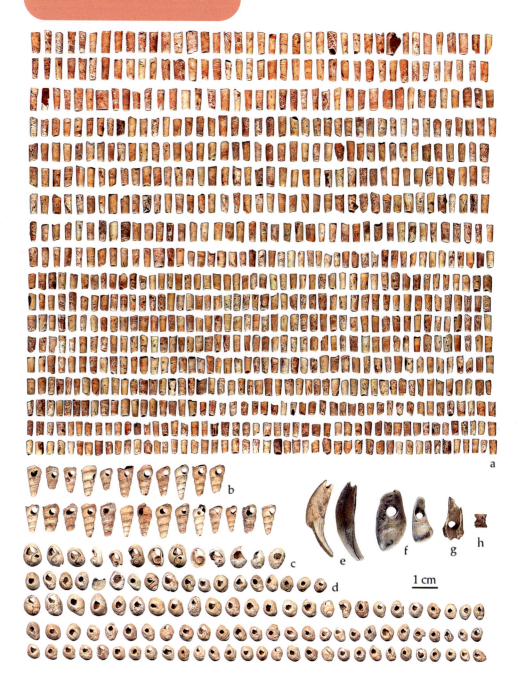

How long do you think it would have taken to make a small child's beaded garment?

Drawing on Rocks and Cave Walls

Among the most spectacular productions of the Ice Age are the many drawings made on rocks in the open air, and also on the walls, ceilings and even floors of caves. In many cases, the artists saw shapes in the rocks which reminded them of different animals, and they then added the parts that were missing. Their art is dominated by animals – mainly horses and bison, but also wild oxen, wild goats, deer, mammoths, etc. Very few humans were drawn (see page 11), but there are lots of strange shapes.

Bison painted on the walls at Covaciella, Spain

Drawing of a doe in red ochre made with finger dots from Covalanas, Spain

There were many ways of making these images. The simplest method was to use fingers to mark cave walls where the surface was soft enough. For harder rocks, or the clay floor, a sharp stone tool was used to make engravings. Drawings were also made with **pigments** – either red (always ochre, or iron oxide) or black (manganese or charcoal). The colour could be applied by natural crayons or it could be crushed into powder and then mixed with water. This could then be applied by brush, pads or by hand. Finally, powdered pigment could also be put in the mouth, mixed with saliva (spit), and then spat onto the wall. This is how the many hand stencils were made: by placing the hand flat against the wall and then spraying it with paint. When the hand is removed, a perfect print of the hand is left.

Many of the images were probably made by adults, – as can be seen from their height above the ground.

However, we know that children were very active in the caves – as can be seen from their footprints (see page 46) – and so it is highly probable that they also made drawings there. In some caves there are fingermarkings on walls and ceilings that were made by small hands. Sometimes the children were clearly lifted up by adults to leave their fingermarks. Stencils of the hands of small children, and even of babies, have also been found. In addition, in some caves there are drawings in small, narrow spaces which no adult could reach – so these must have been made by youngsters.

Drawn in the dark, the cave paintings come alive when lit with the flickering flame of a torch, lamp or fire. The animals seem to move, and so this was like the first cinema, especially if looking at the images also involved storytelling and music.

A hand stencil in Cosquer cave. Such images were made by placing the hand against the cave wall and then spitting or spraying paint at it.

Why would people want to make images inside dark caves?

Was every day a play-day or a school-day for children in the Ice Age?

In hunter-gatherer societies, there is little in the way of teaching with instructions on how to do things. Traditionally, children are encouraged to learn by trial-and-error, by copying older children, or their elders. In this way youngsters gradually acquire their skills by practice.

Children can quickly learn the various methods of chasing, trapping and catching animals through playing and practising with other children. Archaeologists have discovered many small versions of adult tools and weapons that may have been 'working' toys for children.

Hunter-gatherers rarely leave their children behind, and prefer to include them in all their activities away from home. The view that only boys and fathers go on hunting trips together seems old-fashioned these days and, more importantly, the evidence does not support this idea. During the Ice Age all children needed to learn vital life skills in order to survive, so would have joined their family members in all outdoor and indoor activities.

Do you think it is easier for parents today to bring up their children?

SKILLS THAT ICE AGE CHILDREN NEEDED TO LEARN:

- how to make and use tools,
- light a fire,
- find suitable shelter,
- read the behaviour of animals and avoid predators,
- read the surrounding landscape and various weather patterns,
- follow growing seasons and plant life

All of these would have been vital lessons. Children would learn to track animals using signs, scents and sounds, and miniature weapons.

Young adults would also have needed to learn how to make tools – and someone would have had to teach them. There are many **ethnographic** examples of indigenous/first nation men and women carrying their own tools in a leather bag around their waist – it is probably safe to assume that this was also something they did during the Ice Age.

Human children mature slowly, and are dependent on their mothers and the extended family for support, not only for food, but also to teach them the many skills required for their survival. They also needed to find their own way through the landscape, and especially be taught how to avoid any dangers!

Children's footprints in Niaux cave, France

Did children learn to swim in the Ice Age? We don't know, of course, but when people saw animals swimming across rivers, they may have seen it as a quick way to get across the water and given it a try. Also, as they needed to catch fish in fast-flowing rivers, and collected seafood on the seashore, it's probable they used small boats. Since sailing comes with the risk of falling in the water, they may have learned to swim.

> *Do you think Ice Age people swam and washed in rivers when the weather was at its warmest?*
>
> *What would swimming in heavy skin clothing have been like?*

Children were almost certainly taught from an early age to avoid touching and playing with dangerous objects, just the same as today. However, very young children growing up in the Ice Age may have been allowed to handle sharp tools and learn how to use them. The hunter-gatherer Hadza communities of Tanzania in Africa believe that children *learn for themselves* what is dangerous, and they allow very young children – even as young as two or three – to handle sharp knives and blades, because tools are part of a **forager**'s world in Hadza culture. As a result, children quickly become good at using tools because they are allowed to play with them from an early age.

> *Do you think it is a good idea for children to use sharp tools? Would you let someone younger than you play with a sharp object?*

Did children have toys to play with?

At the cave of Le Mas d'Azil in the French Pyrenees, archaeologists recovered a circular disc of bone with an engraved image of a man and bear. It has a hole in the middle, presumably for a cord. When this was pulled, the disc would spin, and the image would seem to move. One can only imagine how thrilling these whizzing visuals must have been, and perhaps not just for children but all the family! Other objects that have been discovered that may have been miniature weapons and playthings include the small ivory spears found in the children's grave at Sunghir. Several small ivory figurines of animals and birds, and a figure of a bear or a 'Lion-man', have been found in the Swabian Alps in Germany. Any toys made of wood, plant material or feathers would have decayed over such a huge time period.

Children living in the Ice Age probably collected **curiosities** like animal bones, feathers, pebbles, fossils and shells. Children and adults often gather natural items from the landscape like stones, rocks, shells, or even things such as leaves and insects. Indeed, it seems to be a human trait

Above: Bear or 'Lion-man' ivory figurine
Below: Brno ivory puppet

Maininskaya clay figure

to collect things and sort them into groups or categories of a similar type. They may have also collected small creatures and kept them as pets.

What sorts of things have you found in nature that you found fun to collect?

Hundreds of children's footprints have been found deep inside caves in France. It seems that even very young children were not afraid to explore the narrow, twisted corridors, climb up narrow chimneys and find their way around these dark and challenging places. Inside Fontanet cave in France there are traces of children throwing small clay balls at each other, and in the same cave a child of about five left knee and handprints while following a puppy or a fox deep into the back of the cave. It is of course possible that the children who visited this cave lived a thousand years apart, as we know caves like Fontanet were visited time and again over thousands of years.

At the far end of Le Tuc d'Audoubert cave in France are the famous clay bison (shown on the next page). Nearby, in the chamber where the clay was collected, there are at least 183 heelprints, from children or adolescents probably playing together under a low ceiling.

Bone disc found at Le Mas d'Azil, France

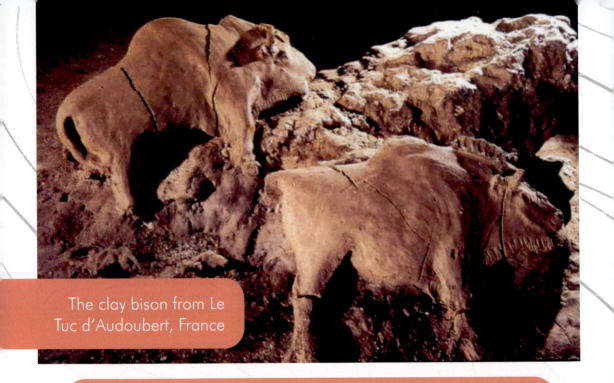

The clay bison from Le Tuc d'Audoubert, France

Do you think the clay sculptures found in caves were made by adults or children?

Another form of entertainment for children may have been the painted animals on cave walls – these images almost come alive when seen by the flickering light from fires, from burning torches made of twigs, or from hand-held lamps made of animal fats. When these low-light sources are moved around the dark chambers, they create shadows that appear to move across the wall with the animals! Cave walls can often glisten with water, and tiny particles (pieces) of the quartz in the calcite rock sparkle when light moves over the surface. In this shadowy context, one can imagine how exciting the 'cinematic' effect of painted animals would have been to our distant ancestors, particularly if accompanied by storytelling and music. Indeed, the effect is no less thrilling for anyone fortunate enough to visit these awesome settings today.

Would you be happy with the toys and games children had in the Ice Age? What would you miss that you use today?

Dogs as hunting aids and pets

Dogs must have gradually **evolved** from wolves towards the end of the Last Ice Age. **Genetically**, both ancient dogs and wolves would not have been like any 'modern' species existing today, and probably looked and behaved differently to the many varieties of dogs (and wolves) that we see around the modern world.

By the end of the Ice Age, or possibly earlier, people had a relationship with dogs, although there is a lot of debate amongst scientists about when, where, and how the change from wolf to dog occurred. We have no idea whether people also used ferrets or birds of prey to hunt, but there is now evidence of early dogs living with humans, and their remains have even been found along with human burials!

Many humans seem to have a deep-rooted fear of wolves, and this has been the case throughout history, with wolves even characterizing as the 'bad guys' in children's stories. This is rather surprising when you think that dogs, related to wolves, are our closest allies. According to many **zoologists**, wolves are not the vicious and dangerous species portrayed in films and legends, but nevertheless there is no denying that they are a top predator. Even a large group of humans with only hand weapons would stand little chance against a pack of wolves and, in the Ice Age, could only escape by climbing trees or taking refuge in a rock shelter or cave.

The frozen puppy known as 'Dogor' around 13,000 years old and found in the permafrost in Siberia in 2018. 'Dogor' is the Yakut word for 'friend.'

One early suggestion of how wolves became domesticated was that hungry wolf cubs started hanging around human camps, scavenging for food, and people selected the friendly ones and killed or drove away the ones they couldn't tame. Regular feeding of these 'strays' may have led to them becoming dependent, and eventually humans and wolves formed a strong relationship that was helpful to both sides.

Tracing of wolf engraving from La Marche (Vienne)

Of course, wolves will not have been the only animals hanging around – a recent study of fox remains found in cave sites of the Swabian Jura in Germany around 40,000 years ago, shows that the foxes were eating a lot of reindeer – doubtless scavenged from carcasses near human camps.

An alternative idea is that groups of human hunters might have encountered wolves that were following the same herds and, recognizing each other's strengths, they began to hunt alongside each other. Perhaps our early ancestors originally learned from wolves how to select the 'easiest pickings' amongst a herd. This may have led to an extended period of co-operation, and later – even much later – a close relationship between the human and wolf developed.

We have at least two theories: the first is that wolves and humans gradually learned to tolerate each other, and a bond eventually developed between the two. The second is that Ice Age people intentionally **domesticated** wolves to be their hunting allies, and to provide protection and companionship, to be a 'back-up' source of meat, and become a useful fur when the animal had no further use.

Which theory do you think is most likely?

How did an ancient wolf become a small chihuahua dog?

HAVING A DOMESTICATED DOG IN THE ICE AGE

But what were the advantages of domestic dogs during the Ice Age? There are surprisingly quite a lot when you think about it!

- Help with hunting, herding and tracking;
- guarding dwellings, children and food;
- protection against predators;
- transporting loads and children;
- companionship and security; bed warmers;
- eating refuse and left-overs;
- entertainment – playfulness in dogs appeals to children and adults alike;
- the status of owning a 'top-dog' – perhaps they were even traded?
- And finally for food and fur pelts.

Both of these situations may have occurred many times over the thousands of years we call the Upper Palaeolithic period of our past. What is certainly probable is that the human and wolf, wolf-dog and human-dog relationship took a very long time to succeed.

A dog's hearing is better than a human's. They can hear four times farther away, and locate the exact location of a sound. A dog's sense of smell is also far better than our own. Arctic people have used dogs for almost as long as they have been living in that part of the world, and archaeological evidence has suggested their presence there for at least 17,000 years.

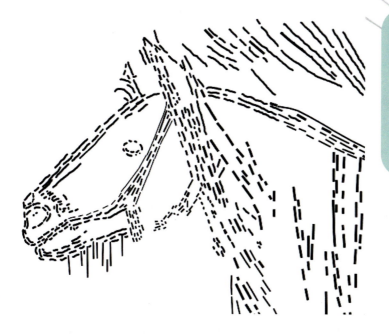

Engraving of a horse with bridle, found in Oxocelhaya cave

Experiments have shown that big dogs are easily taught to carry a large pack strapped to their back, so dogs could have been used to help take Ice Age luggage to another home base. But Ice Age people were so intelligent, and had become so familiar with the behaviour of animals over thousands of years, that they must surely have used horses and reindeer as pack animals, or even to ride. It is very easy to tame foals and fawns, and thus control them throughout their lives. As we have seen, Ice Age people were very mobile and often had to take their heavy tents and other equipment over long distances and often rough terrain. Why would they carry or drag everything themselves when they could easily have horses and reindeer to do it for them? And indeed we have evidence for this, because several Ice age depictions show horses wearing what seem to be simple bridles.

It is also important to remember that people must have sometimes travelled by boat or canoe – even though no such vessel has survived from so long ago, it is obvious that travelling by river would have been far simpler and often more direct than tramping up and down hills!

Are we able to learn anything from our Ice Age ancestors?

1,200 **generations** of human families spanned the 30,000 years we have described in this short book, and we hope you can form some impression of the tough and hardy people who were able to **adapt** to their natural surroundings, and who did everything they could to make sure that their children survived. Archaeologists are learning a great many things about early peoples as they continue to gather new evidence about our deep past – especially in areas where, unfortunately, climate change is causing ice and **permafrost** to melt at an alarming rate. Of course, we will never know what early humans thought and believed about either their origins, or the world in which they lived. However, we hope we have provided you with a clearer picture of the kind of 'everyday lives' early **hunter-gatherers** experienced, and some of the many challenges they faced.

We hope this book has taken you back in time, and given you an idea of what our ancient ancestors

Reconstruction of a group of Ice Age people

were like, and how they lived from day to day. In the future it is likely that archaeologists and scientists will discover a lot more about Ice Age cultures.

We have described the men, women and children who lived for around 30,000 years in Ice Age Europe, and are the direct ancestors of many people alive today.

Ice Age people must have worked together to overcome many difficult challenges, like a changing climate and food shortages. Yet through their determination they managed to rear their children to adulthood. Without their resolve and sense of purpose, the human species would not have survived. We have a great deal to thank them for.

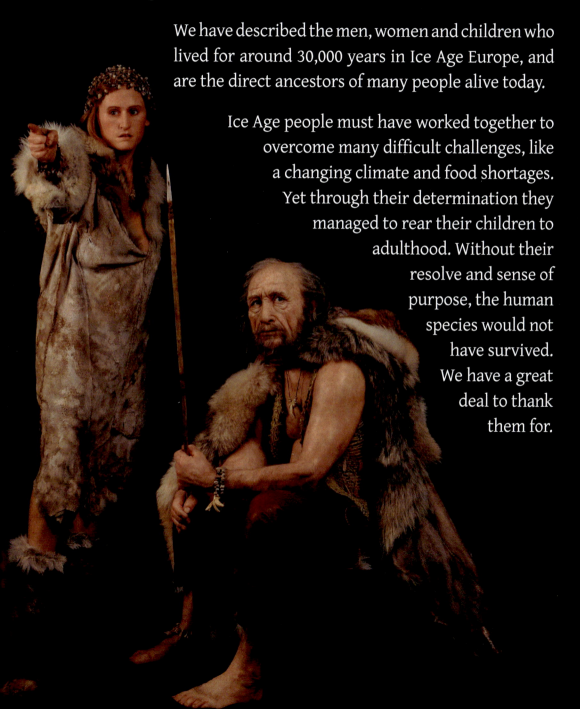

Archaeological Methods

Archaeologists are people who study the past by digging up (excavating) areas where people have lived. Excavations cut down through many layers of time, especially in places where people have lived for centuries or thousands of years, which means finding objects from many different periods. Working out how old they are, who might have made and used them, and what they were for is a large part of archaeology.

Figuring out how old something is that has been excavated can be challenging, but archaeologists have various ways of doing this. Figuring out the age of something is called **dating**. The most common dating method is to inspect the object and see what it is similar to, basing the search on a wide range of other evidence from excavations. Then the object is categorised with similar objects based on its material, shape, the way it was made and other details about it. This is called making a typology. Once a series of things are built up and from each period of time and place, they can act a bit like a tape-measure for time, where you can put the newly excavated object on the part of the timeline near the objects that are most similar to it. This method is used for certain types of archaeological objects made by humans that there are many of, including stone tools and pottery. It doesn't work so well for rare or unique items that don't have many comparisons.

Another common way of finding out the age of a site is radiocarbon dating. This type of dating can be used on things that were once alive, such as wood, seeds, and bones. During their lives, all plants and animals naturally absorb the radioactive isotope carbon-14 (^{14}C) into their cells, but once they die the cells don't take any more in. Radiocarbon dating uses laboratory equipment to analyse the ^{14}C left in the material (such as in the wood charcoal left from a fire), and this measurement can be used to estimate its age. Dating a few different materials from an archaeological site using this method can give a good general idea of how old the site is, and how long it was used for.

Excavation at Cueva Antón, Murcia, Spain

Other scientific methods are used in archaeological work too: ancient human bones (osteoarchaeology), ancient animal bones (zooarchaeology), ancient plants (archaeobotany or palaeobotany), and DNA (palaeogenetics). Analysing excavated soil (sediment) can help archaeologists find traces of things that you can no longer see, such as plant pollen grains, animal skins, or ancient parasites.

Glossary

Adapt/adaptation: the process of changing to suit different conditions.

Antibodies: proteins produced in the blood that fight diseases by attacking and killing harmful bacteria, viruses, etc.

Antiseptic: A substance that prevents infection by killing germs and microorganisms on the surfaces of the body (skin).

Archaeologist: a person who works to understand the past by digging up (excavating) and studying the things left behind by past people.

Biologically modern humans: us! Also known as *Homo sapiens* or *H. sapiens*.

Cradleboard: a flat board or frame to which an infant is strapped, making it easy for an adult to carry.

Curing or tanning animal skins: the process of treating the skins and hides of animals to produce leather.

Curiosities: unusual or interesting objects.

Dating: using archaeological methods to figure out how old something is.

Debris: rubbish or broken items.

Domestication: something wild changing to become more suitable for humans. Examples include wolves evolving into dogs by interacting with humans, or plants changing over time due to being grown or harvested by humans.

Ethnography: the scientific study of peoples and cultures with their language, customs, habits and way of life.

Evolved: having developed through a gradual process.

Extinction: a situation in which something no longer exists.

Fibrous: something made of many threads (fibres), and usually quite tough.

Foraging/forager: The activity of finding, gathering and harvesting wild foods and searching for things that you use, like firewood. A forager is a person who forages.

Fungal infections: any diseases or conditions caused by a fungus.

Generation: all the people of about the same age within a society or within a particular family.

Genetically: In a way that relates to origin or development. Genetics is the study of how physical traits and characteristics are passed from one generation to the next.

Genetic mutation: a mistake or a permanent alteration in the DNA sequence - a chain of chemical units found in each cell of living things. DNA is the material that carries all the information about how a living thing will look and function.

Grave goods: items either buried with a body, or left near a grave. These may have been the belongings of the person who died, or gifts from their community.

Hunter-gatherer lifestyle: A way of living that relies on hunting and fishing and foraging for wild vegetation and nutrients necessary for survival. Until around 12,000 years ago when humans began farming, all humans practised hunter-gathering.

Immune system: the cells and tissues in the body that make it able to protect itself against infection.

Indigenous/first nation people: the people who originally lived in a place (e.g. a country) rather than people who moved into a place.

Iodine: a chemical element that is found in small amounts in seawater and seaweed and is used to prevent infection.

Lice/louse: a small insect that lives on the bodies or in the hair of people and animals.

Migration: the process of animals or people travelling to a different place, usually when the seasons change.

Parasitic infection: any small organism, such as a virus or bacterium that can cause disease.

Pathogens: Pathogens or germs cause infectious diseases once they have entered the body. Pathogens include viruses, bacteria, fungi, and protozoans.

Permafrost: Permafrost is a permanently frozen layer on the Earth's surface. It consists of soil, gravel, and sand, usually bound together with ice.

Pigments: ochre (iron oxide) and manganese are types of minerals used by people to paint and draw. When they are used for this purpose, we call them pigments. Charcoal was also a commonly used pigment.

Putrefied matter: organic matter that has decayed, usually producing a strong unpleasant smell.

Shuttle, smoother and spatula: Bone or stone tools with a broad thin blade used for processing and working animal skins.

Soil or sediment sample: A small amount of excavated dirt from a known location within an archaeological dig, removed carefully in order to be analysed in a laboratory.

Thermal protection: clothing that traps warm air between the skin and the outer garments providing insulation against cold conditions.

Tuber: a thick part of a plant's stem and root system that grows underground. Some types of tubers can be eaten by humans.

Zoologist: a person who scientifically studies animals.

Questions

Would you have enjoyed learning the skills you'd need to make food in the Ice Age?

Would you rather hunt for and gather your food every day or go to the supermarket?

If our Ice Age ancestors had a word for smelly, what do you think it would be?

Do you think we are all too clean? Would you prefer to wash less?

It is unlikely that people in distant communities spoke the same language, so do you think they may have shared a 'sign' language or other ways that helped them communicate with each other?

Would you have enjoyed making your own clothes in the Ice Age rather than buying them like we do today?

Do you think beads were worn every day, or only for special occasions like ceremonies, or only for burial?

Do you believe that lucky charms can stop bad things from happening?

How long do you think it would have taken to make a small child's beaded garment?

Why would people want to make images inside dark caves?

Do you think it is easier for parents today to bring up their children?

Do you think Ice Age people swam and washed in rivers when the weather was at its warmest?

What would swimming in heavy skin clothing have been like?

Do you think it is a good idea for children to use sharp tools? Would you let someone younger than you play with a sharp object?

What sorts of things have you found in nature that you found fun to collect?

Do you think the clay sculptures found in caves were made by adults or children?

Would you be happy with the toys and games children had in the Ice Age? What would you miss that you use today?

How did an ancient wolf become a small chihuahua dog?

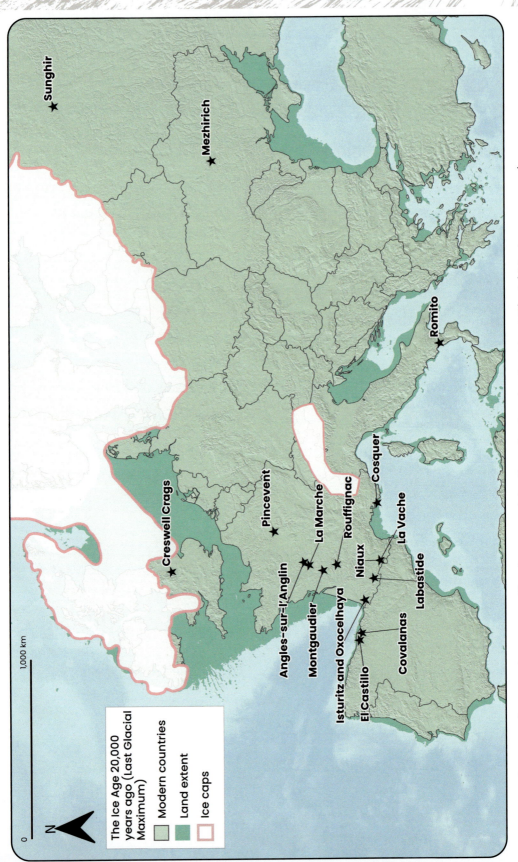

Map of Europe showing the extent of land mass and the Eurasian ice sheets at Last Glacial Maximum around 20,000 years ago.

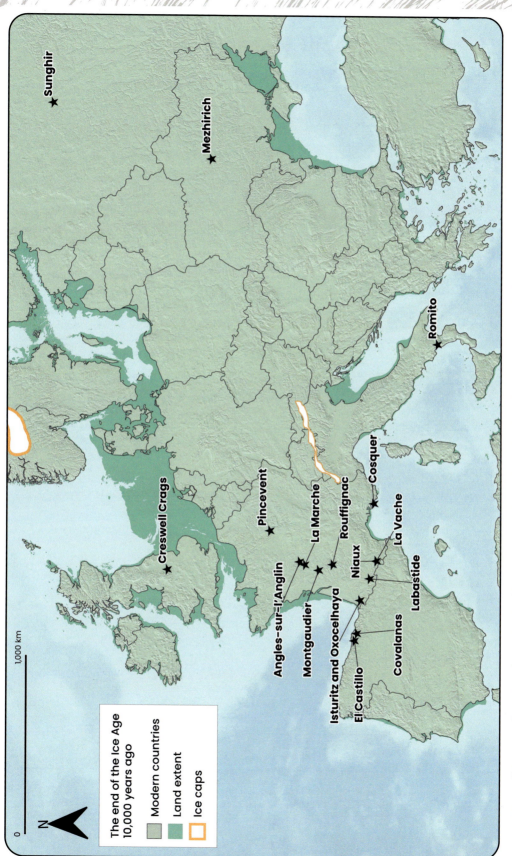

Map of Europe showing the extent of land mass and the Eurasian ice sheets at the end of the Ice Age around 10,000 years ago.